THIS BOOK BELONGS TO:

CONTACT INFORMATION	
NAME	
ADDRESS	
PHONE #	
EMAIL	

Copyright © Teresa Rother
All rights reserved. No part of this publication may be reproduced, distributed, or transmitted in any form or by any means, including photocopy, recording, or other electronic or mechanical methods.

DEDICATION

This Prepper Log Book is dedicated to survivalists and preppers who want to track and record supplies and inventory for off-grid and wilderness living.

You are my inspiration for producing this book and I'm honored to be a part of your record-keeping and organization.

HOW TO USE THIS BOOK

This Preppers Log Book will help you by accurately planning, recording, and organizing your information.

Here are examples of information for you to fill in and write the details of your logbook.

Fill in the following information:

1. Contact list - Record important contact information.
2. Bug Out Bag Checklist - Jot down the items you need for evacuations and emergencies.
3. Outdoor Survival Checklist - Jot down needed supplies for a wilderness, hunting, or fishing trip.
4. Shopping List - Add grocery items needed.
5. Food Inventory - Record date, category, food item, expiration date, size, and units.
6. Garden Log - Record plant name, date planted, soil amendments, harvest date, prep and storage.
7. Log - Track equipment, date, maintenance/service repair, and cost.
8. Water Filtration System Log - Track equipment, date, maintenance/service repair, and cost.
9. Heating System Log - Track equipment, date, maintenance/service repair, and cost.
10. Energy System - Track equipment, date, maintenance/service repair, and cost.
11. Gun Inventory - Record gun brand and manufacturer, serial number, date, and cost
12. Ammo Inventory - Record ammo brand and manufacturer, caliber/gauge, quantity, and date

CONTACT LIST

CONTACT INFORMATION	
NAME	
ADDRESS	
PHONE #	
EMAIL	

CONTACT INFORMATION	
NAME	
ADDRESS	
PHONE #	
EMAIL	

CONTACT INFORMATION	
NAME	
ADDRESS	
PHONE #	
EMAIL	

CONTACT INFORMATION	
NAME	
ADDRESS	
PHONE #	
EMAIL	

CONTACT INFORMATION	
NAME	
ADDRESS	
PHONE #	
EMAIL	

CONTACT INFORMATION	
NAME	
ADDRESS	
PHONE #	
EMAIL	

CONTACT LIST

CONTACT INFORMATION	
NAME	
ADDRESS	
PHONE #	
EMAIL	

CONTACT INFORMATION	
NAME	
ADDRESS	
PHONE #	
EMAIL	

CONTACT INFORMATION	
NAME	
ADDRESS	
PHONE #	
EMAIL	

CONTACT INFORMATION	
NAME	
ADDRESS	
PHONE #	
EMAIL	

CONTACT INFORMATION	
NAME	
ADDRESS	
PHONE #	
EMAIL	

CONTACT INFORMATION	
NAME	
ADDRESS	
PHONE #	
EMAIL	

CONTACT LIST

CONTACT INFORMATION	
NAME	
ADDRESS	
PHONE #	
EMAIL	

CONTACT INFORMATION	
NAME	
ADDRESS	
PHONE #	
EMAIL	

CONTACT INFORMATION	
NAME	
ADDRESS	
PHONE #	
EMAIL	

CONTACT INFORMATION	
NAME	
ADDRESS	
PHONE #	
EMAIL	

CONTACT INFORMATION	
NAME	
ADDRESS	
PHONE #	
EMAIL	

CONTACT INFORMATION	
NAME	
ADDRESS	
PHONE #	
EMAIL	

CONTACT LIST

CONTACT INFORMATION	
NAME	
ADDRESS	
PHONE #	
EMAIL	

CONTACT INFORMATION	
NAME	
ADDRESS	
PHONE #	
EMAIL	

CONTACT INFORMATION	
NAME	
ADDRESS	
PHONE #	
EMAIL	

CONTACT INFORMATION	
NAME	
ADDRESS	
PHONE #	
EMAIL	

CONTACT INFORMATION	
NAME	
ADDRESS	
PHONE #	
EMAIL	

CONTACT INFORMATION	
NAME	
ADDRESS	
PHONE #	
EMAIL	

BUG OUT BAG CHECKLIST

SUPPLY LIST	SUPPLY LIST
☐ water	☐
☐ food supplies	☐
☐ medication	☐
☐ first aid kit	☐
☐ tent/shelter	☐
☐ blankets/sleeping bag	☐
☐ fishing/hunting gear	☐
☐ batteries	☐
☐ radio	☐
☐ matches/fire starter kit	☐
☐ duct tape	☐
☐ paracord	☐
☐ cold weather clothes	☐
☐	☐
☐	☐
☐	☐
☐	☐
☐	☐
☐	☐
☐	☐
☐	☐
☐	☐
☐	☐
☐	☐
☐	☐
☐	☐
☐	☐
☐	☐
☐	☐

BUG OUT BAG CHECKLIST

SUPPLY LIST	SUPPLY LIST
☐	☐
☐	☐
☐	☐
☐	☐
☐	☐
☐	☐
☐	☐
☐	☐
☐	☐
☐	☐
☐	☐
☐	☐
☐	☐
☐	☐
☐	☐
☐	☐
☐	☐
☐	☐
☐	☐
☐	☐
☐	☐
☐	☐
☐	☐
☐	☐
☐	☐
☐	☐
☐	☐
☐	☐
☐	☐
☐	☐

OUTDOOR SURVIVAL CHECKLIST

SUPPLY LIST	SUPPLY LIST
☐ water	☐
☐ food supplies	☐
☐ medication	☐
☐ first aid kit	☐
☐ tent/shelter	☐
☐ hunting gear	☐
☐ fishing gear	☐
☐ batteries	☐
☐ radio	☐
☐ paracord	☐
☐ duct tape	☐
☐ cold weather clothes	☐
☐ raincoat	☐
☐ matches/fire starter	☐
☐ flashlight/head lamp	☐
☐ compass/GPS tracking system	☐
☐ multipurpose tool	☐
☐ shovel	☐
☐ axe	☐
☐ paracord	☐
☐ knife	☐
☐ pepper spray	☐
☐	☐
☐	☐
☐	☐
☐	☐
☐	☐
☐	☐
☐	☐

OUTDOOR SURVIVAL CHECKLIST

SUPPLY LIST	SUPPLY LIST
☐	☐
☐	☐
☐	☐
☐	☐
☐	☐
☐	☐
☐	☐
☐	☐
☐	☐
☐	☐
☐	☐
☐	☐
☐	☐
☐	☐
☐	☐
☐	☐
☐	☐
☐	☐
☐	☐
☐	☐
☐	☐
☐	☐
☐	☐
☐	☐
☐	☐
☐	☐
☐	☐
☐	☐
☐	☐
☐	☐

SHOPPING LIST

MEAT/CANNED FISH	DRIED GOODS
☐	☐
☐	☐
☐	☐
☐	☐
☐	☐
☐	☐
☐	☐
☐	☐
☐	☐
☐	☐
☐	☐
☐	☐
☐	☐
☐	☐
☐	☐
☐	☐
☐	☐
☐	☐
☐	☐
☐	☐
☐	☐
☐	☐
☐	☐
☐	☐
☐	☐
☐	☐
☐	☐
☐	☐
☐	☐
☐	☐

SHOPPING LIST

VEGETABLES	CANNED FRUIT
☐	☐
☐	☐
☐	☐
☐	☐
☐	☐
☐	☐
☐	☐
☐	☐
☐	☐
☐	☐
☐	☐
☐	☐
☐	☐
☐	☐
☐	☐
☐	☐
☐	☐
☐	☐
☐	☐
☐	☐
☐	☐
☐	☐
☐	☐
☐	☐
☐	☐
☐	☐
☐	☐
☐	☐
☐	☐
☐	☐

SHOPPING LIST

MEAT/CANNED FISH	DRIED GOODS
☐	☐
☐	☐
☐	☐
☐	☐
☐	☐
☐	☐
☐	☐
☐	☐
☐	☐
☐	☐
☐	☐
☐	☐
☐	☐
☐	☐
☐	☐
☐	☐
☐	☐
☐	☐
☐	☐
☐	☐
☐	☐
☐	☐
☐	☐
☐	☐
☐	☐
☐	☐
☐	☐
☐	☐
☐	☐
☐	☐

SHOPPING LIST

VEGETABLES	CANNED FRUIT
☐	☐
☐	☐
☐	☐
☐	☐
☐	☐
☐	☐
☐	☐
☐	☐
☐	☐
☐	☐
☐	☐
☐	☐
☐	☐
☐	☐
☐	☐
☐	☐
☐	☐
☐	☐
☐	☐
☐	☐
☐	☐
☐	☐
☐	☐
☐	☐
☐	☐
☐	☐
☐	☐
☐	☐
☐	☐
☐	☐

SHOPPING LIST

MEAT/CANNED FISH	DRIED GOODS
☐	☐
☐	☐
☐	☐
☐	☐
☐	☐
☐	☐
☐	☐
☐	☐
☐	☐
☐	☐
☐	☐
☐	☐
☐	☐
☐	☐
☐	☐
☐	☐
☐	☐
☐	☐
☐	☐
☐	☐
☐	☐
☐	☐
☐	☐
☐	☐
☐	☐
☐	☐
☐	☐
☐	☐
☐	☐
☐	☐

SHOPPING LIST

VEGETABLES	CANNED FRUIT
☐	☐
☐	☐
☐	☐
☐	☐
☐	☐
☐	☐
☐	☐
☐	☐
☐	☐
☐	☐
☐	☐
☐	☐
☐	☐
☐	☐
☐	☐
☐	☐
☐	☐
☐	☐
☐	☐
☐	☐
☐	☐
☐	☐
☐	☐
☐	☐
☐	☐
☐	☐
☐	☐
☐	☐
☐	☐

SHOPPING LIST

MEAT/CANNED FISH	DRIED GOODS
☐	☐
☐	☐
☐	☐
☐	☐
☐	☐
☐	☐
☐	☐
☐	☐
☐	☐
☐	☐
☐	☐
☐	☐
☐	☐
☐	☐
☐	☐
☐	☐
☐	☐
☐	☐
☐	☐
☐	☐
☐	☐
☐	☐
☐	☐
☐	☐
☐	☐
☐	☐
☐	☐
☐	☐
☐	☐

SHOPPING LIST

VEGETABLES	CANNED FRUIT
☐	☐
☐	☐
☐	☐
☐	☐
☐	☐
☐	☐
☐	☐
☐	☐
☐	☐
☐	☐
☐	☐
☐	☐
☐	☐
☐	☐
☐	☐
☐	☐
☐	☐
☐	☐
☐	☐
☐	☐
☐	☐
☐	☐
☐	☐
☐	☐
☐	☐
☐	☐
☐	☐
☐	☐
☐	☐
☐	☐

SHOPPING LIST

MEAT/CANNED FISH	DRIED GOODS
☐	☐
☐	☐
☐	☐
☐	☐
☐	☐
☐	☐
☐	☐
☐	☐
☐	☐
☐	☐
☐	☐
☐	☐
☐	☐
☐	☐
☐	☐
☐	☐
☐	☐
☐	☐
☐	☐
☐	☐
☐	☐
☐	☐
☐	☐
☐	☐
☐	☐
☐	☐
☐	☐
☐	☐
☐	☐
☐	☐
☐	☐

SHOPPING LIST

VEGETABLES	CANNED FRUIT
☐	☐
☐	☐
☐	☐
☐	☐
☐	☐
☐	☐
☐	☐
☐	☐
☐	☐
☐	☐
☐	☐
☐	☐
☐	☐
☐	☐
☐	☐
☐	☐
☐	☐
☐	☐
☐	☐
☐	☐
☐	☐
☐	☐
☐	☐
☐	☐
☐	☐
☐	☐
☐	☐
☐	☐
☐	☐
☐	☐
☐	☐

SHOPPING LIST

MEAT/CANNED FISH	DRIED GOODS
☐	☐
☐	☐
☐	☐
☐	☐
☐	☐
☐	☐
☐	☐
☐	☐
☐	☐
☐	☐
☐	☐
☐	☐
☐	☐
☐	☐
☐	☐
☐	☐
☐	☐
☐	☐
☐	☐
☐	☐
☐	☐
☐	☐
☐	☐
☐	☐
☐	☐
☐	☐
☐	☐
☐	☐
☐	☐
☐	☐
☐	☐

SHOPPING LIST

VEGETABLES	CANNED FRUIT
☐	☐
☐	☐
☐	☐
☐	☐
☐	☐
☐	☐
☐	☐
☐	☐
☐	☐
☐	☐
☐	☐
☐	☐
☐	☐
☐	☐
☐	☐
☐	☐
☐	☐
☐	☐
☐	☐
☐	☐
☐	☐
☐	☐
☐	☐
☐	☐
☐	☐
☐	☐
☐	☐
☐	☐
☐	☐
☐	☐
☐	☐

SHOPPING LIST

MEAT/CANNED FISH	DRIED GOODS
☐	☐
☐	☐
☐	☐
☐	☐
☐	☐
☐	☐
☐	☐
☐	☐
☐	☐
☐	☐
☐	☐
☐	☐
☐	☐
☐	☐
☐	☐
☐	☐
☐	☐
☐	☐
☐	☐
☐	☐
☐	☐
☐	☐
☐	☐
☐	☐
☐	☐
☐	☐
☐	☐
☐	☐

SHOPPING LIST

VEGETABLES	CANNED FRUIT
☐	☐
☐	☐
☐	☐
☐	☐
☐	☐
☐	☐
☐	☐
☐	☐
☐	☐
☐	☐
☐	☐
☐	☐
☐	☐
☐	☐
☐	☐
☐	☐
☐	☐
☐	☐
☐	☐
☐	☐
☐	☐
☐	☐
☐	☐
☐	☐
☐	☐
☐	☐
☐	☐
☐	☐
☐	☐
☐	☐

SHOPPING LIST

MEAT/CANNED FISH	DRIED GOODS
☐	☐
☐	☐
☐	☐
☐	☐
☐	☐
☐	☐
☐	☐
☐	☐
☐	☐
☐	☐
☐	☐
☐	☐
☐	☐
☐	☐
☐	☐
☐	☐
☐	☐
☐	☐
☐	☐
☐	☐
☐	☐
☐	☐
☐	☐
☐	☐
☐	☐
☐	☐
☐	☐
☐	☐
☐	☐
☐	☐

SHOPPING LIST

VEGETABLES	CANNED FRUIT
☐	☐
☐	☐
☐	☐
☐	☐
☐	☐
☐	☐
☐	☐
☐	☐
☐	☐
☐	☐
☐	☐
☐	☐
☐	☐
☐	☐
☐	☐
☐	☐
☐	☐
☐	☐
☐	☐
☐	☐
☐	☐
☐	☐
☐	☐
☐	☐
☐	☐
☐	☐
☐	☐
☐	☐
☐	☐

SHOPPING LIST

MEAT/CANNED FISH	DRIED GOODS
☐	☐
☐	☐
☐	☐
☐	☐
☐	☐
☐	☐
☐	☐
☐	☐
☐	☐
☐	☐
☐	☐
☐	☐
☐	☐
☐	☐
☐	☐
☐	☐
☐	☐
☐	☐
☐	☐
☐	☐
☐	☐
☐	☐
☐	☐
☐	☐
☐	☐
☐	☐
☐	☐
☐	☐
☐	☐
☐	☐

SHOPPING LIST

VEGETABLES	CANNED FRUIT
☐	☐
☐	☐
☐	☐
☐	☐
☐	☐
☐	☐
☐	☐
☐	☐
☐	☐
☐	☐
☐	☐
☐	☐
☐	☐
☐	☐
☐	☐
☐	☐
☐	☐
☐	☐
☐	☐
☐	☐
☐	☐
☐	☐
☐	☐
☐	☐
☐	☐
☐	☐
☐	☐
☐	☐
☐	☐
☐	☐

SHOPPING LIST

MEAT/CANNED FISH	DRIED GOODS
☐	☐
☐	☐
☐	☐
☐	☐
☐	☐
☐	☐
☐	☐
☐	☐
☐	☐
☐	☐
☐	☐
☐	☐
☐	☐
☐	☐
☐	☐
☐	☐
☐	☐
☐	☐
☐	☐
☐	☐
☐	☐
☐	☐
☐	☐
☐	☐
☐	☐
☐	☐
☐	☐
☐	☐
☐	☐

SHOPPING LIST

VEGETABLES	CANNED FRUIT
☐	☐
☐	☐
☐	☐
☐	☐
☐	☐
☐	☐
☐	☐
☐	☐
☐	☐
☐	☐
☐	☐
☐	☐
☐	☐
☐	☐
☐	☐
☐	☐
☐	☐
☐	☐
☐	☐
☐	☐
☐	☐
☐	☐
☐	☐
☐	☐
☐	☐
☐	☐
☐	☐
☐	☐
☐	☐
☐	☐

FOOD INVENTORY

DATE	CATEGORY	FOOD ITEM	EXP. DATE	SIZE	UNITS

FOOD INVENTORY

DATE	CATEGORY	FOOD ITEM	EXP. DATE	SIZE	UNITS

FOOD INVENTORY

DATE	CATEGORY	FOOD ITEM	EXP. DATE	SIZE	UNITS

FOOD INVENTORY

DATE	CATEGORY	FOOD ITEM	EXP. DATE	SIZE	UNITS

FOOD INVENTORY

DATE	CATEGORY	FOOD ITEM	EXP. DATE	SIZE	UNITS

FOOD INVENTORY

DATE	CATEGORY	FOOD ITEM	EXP. DATE	SIZE	UNITS

FOOD INVENTORY

DATE	CATEGORY	FOOD ITEM	EXP. DATE	SIZE	UNITS

FOOD INVENTORY

DATE	CATEGORY	FOOD ITEM	EXP. DATE	SIZE	UNITS

FOOD INVENTORY

DATE	CATEGORY	FOOD ITEM	EXP. DATE	SIZE	UNITS

FOOD INVENTORY

DATE	CATEGORY	FOOD ITEM	EXP. DATE	SIZE	UNITS

FOOD INVENTORY

DATE	CATEGORY	FOOD ITEM	EXP. DATE	SIZE	UNITS

FOOD INVENTORY

DATE	CATEGORY	FOOD ITEM	EXP. DATE	SIZE	UNITS

FOOD INVENTORY

DATE	CATEGORY	FOOD ITEM	EXP. DATE	SIZE	UNITS

FOOD INVENTORY

DATE	CATEGORY	FOOD ITEM	EXP. DATE	SIZE	UNITS

FOOD INVENTORY

DATE	CATEGORY	FOOD ITEM	EXP. DATE	SIZE	UNITS

FOOD INVENTORY

DATE	CATEGORY	FOOD ITEM	EXP. DATE	SIZE	UNITS

FOOD INVENTORY

DATE	CATEGORY	FOOD ITEM	EXP. DATE	SIZE	UNITS

FOOD INVENTORY

DATE	CATEGORY	FOOD ITEM	EXP. DATE	SIZE	UNITS

FOOD INVENTORY

DATE	CATEGORY	FOOD ITEM	EXP. DATE	SIZE	UNITS

FOOD INVENTORY

DATE	CATEGORY	FOOD ITEM	EXP. DATE	SIZE	UNITS

FOOD INVENTORY

DATE	CATEGORY	FOOD ITEM	EXP. DATE	SIZE	UNITS

FOOD INVENTORY

DATE	CATEGORY	FOOD ITEM	EXP. DATE	SIZE	UNITS

FOOD INVENTORY

DATE	CATEGORY	FOOD ITEM	EXP. DATE	SIZE	UNITS

FOOD INVENTORY

DATE	CATEGORY	FOOD ITEM	EXP. DATE	SIZE	UNITS

FOOD INVENTORY

DATE	CATEGORY	FOOD ITEM	EXP. DATE	SIZE	UNITS

FOOD INVENTORY

DATE	CATEGORY	FOOD ITEM	EXP. DATE	SIZE	UNITS

FOOD INVENTORY

DATE	CATEGORY	FOOD ITEM	EXP. DATE	SIZE	UNITS

FOOD INVENTORY

DATE	CATEGORY	FOOD ITEM	EXP. DATE	SIZE	UNITS

FOOD INVENTORY

DATE	CATEGORY	FOOD ITEM	EXP. DATE	SIZE	UNITS

FOOD INVENTORY

DATE	CATEGORY	FOOD ITEM	EXP. DATE	SIZE	UNITS

GARDEN LOG

PLANT NAME	DATE PLANTED	SOIL AMENDMENTS	HARVEST DATE	PREP AND STORAGE

GARDEN LOG

PLANT NAME	DATE PLANTED	SOIL AMENDMENTS	HARVEST DATE	PREP AND STORAGE

GARDEN LOG

PLANT NAME	DATE PLANTED	SOIL AMENDMENTS	HARVEST DATE	PREP AND STORAGE

GARDEN LOG

PLANT NAME	DATE PLANTED	SOIL AMENDMENTS	HARVEST DATE	PREP AND STORAGE

GARDEN LOG

PLANT NAME	DATE PLANTED	SOIL AMENDMENTS	HARVEST DATE	PREP AND STORAGE

GARDEN LOG

PLANT NAME	DATE PLANTED	SOIL AMENDMENTS	HARVEST DATE	PREP AND STORAGE

GARDEN LOG

PLANT NAME	DATE PLANTED	SOIL AMENDMENTS	HARVEST DATE	PREP AND STORAGE

GARDEN LOG

PLANT NAME	DATE PLANTED	SOIL AMENDMENTS	HARVEST DATE	PREP AND STORAGE

GARDEN LOG

PLANT NAME	DATE PLANTED	SOIL AMENDMENTS	HARVEST DATE	PREP AND STORAGE

GARDEN LOG

PLANT NAME	DATE PLANTED	SOIL AMENDMENTS	HARVEST DATE	PREP AND STORAGE

GARDEN LOG

PLANT NAME	DATE PLANTED	SOIL AMENDMENTS	HARVEST DATE	PREP AND STORAGE

GARDEN LOG

PLANT NAME	DATE PLANTED	SOIL AMENDMENTS	HARVEST DATE	PREP AND STORAGE

GARDEN LOG

PLANT NAME	DATE PLANTED	SOIL AMENDMENTS	HARVEST DATE	PREP AND STORAGE

GARDEN LOG

PLANT NAME	DATE PLANTED	SOIL AMENDMENTS	HARVEST DATE	PREP AND STORAGE

GARDEN LOG

PLANT NAME	DATE PLANTED	SOIL AMENDMENTS	HARVEST DATE	PREP AND STORAGE

GARDEN LOG

PLANT NAME	DATE PLANTED	SOIL AMENDMENTS	HARVEST DATE	PREP AND STORAGE

GARDEN LOG

PLANT NAME	DATE PLANTED	SOIL AMENDMENTS	HARVEST DATE	PREP AND STORAGE

GARDEN LOG

PLANT NAME	DATE PLANTED	SOIL AMENDMENTS	HARVEST DATE	PREP AND STORAGE

GARDEN LOG

PLANT NAME	DATE PLANTED	SOIL AMENDMENTS	HARVEST DATE	PREP AND STORAGE

EQUIPMENT LOG

EQUIPMENT	DATE	MAINTENANCE/SERVICE REPAIR	COST

EQUIPMENT LOG

EQUIPMENT	DATE	MAINTENANCE/SERVICE REPAIR	COST

EQUIPMENT LOG

EQUIPMENT	DATE	MAINTENANCE/SERVICE REPAIR	COST

EQUIPMENT LOG

EQUIPMENT	DATE	MAINTENANCE/SERVICE REPAIR	COST

EQUIPMENT LOG

EQUIPMENT	DATE	MAINTENANCE/SERVICE REPAIR	COST

WATER & FILTRATION SYSTEM LOG

EQUIPMENT	DATE	MAINTENANCE/SERVICE REPAIR	COST

WATER & FILTRATION SYSTEM LOG

EQUIPMENT	DATE	MAINTENANCE/SERVICE REPAIR	COST

WATER & FILTRATION SYSTEM LOG

EQUIPMENT	DATE	MAINTENANCE/SERVICE REPAIR	COST

WATER & FILTRATION SYSTEM LOG

EQUIPMENT	DATE	MAINTENANCE/SERVICE REPAIR	COST

WATER & FILTRATION SYSTEM LOG

EQUIPMENT	DATE	MAINTENANCE/SERVICE REPAIR	COST

HEATING SYSTEM LOG

EQUIPMENT	DATE	MAINTENANCE/SERVICE REPAIR	COST

HEATING SYSTEM LOG

EQUIPMENT	DATE	MAINTENANCE/SERVICE REPAIR	COST

HEATING SYSTEM LOG

EQUIPMENT	DATE	MAINTENANCE/SERVICE REPAIR	COST

HEATING SYSTEM LOG

EQUIPMENT	DATE	MAINTENANCE/SERVICE REPAIR	COST

HEATING SYSTEM LOG

EQUIPMENT	DATE	MAINTENANCE/SERVICE REPAIR	COST

ENERGY SYSTEM LOG

EQUIPMENT	DATE	MAINTENANCE/SERVICE REPAIR	COST

ENERGY SYSTEM LOG

EQUIPMENT	DATE	MAINTENANCE/SERVICE REPAIR	COST

ENERGY SYSTEM LOG

EQUIPMENT	DATE	MAINTENANCE/SERVICE REPAIR	COST

GUN INVENTORY

GUN BRAND/MANUFACTURER	SERIAL NUMBER	DATE	COST

GUN INVENTORY

GUN BRAND/MANUFACTURER	SERIAL NUMBER	DATE	COST

AMMO INVENTORY

AMMO BRAND/MANUFACTURER	CALIBER/GAUGE	QUANTITY	DATE

AMMO INVENTORY

AMMO BRAND/MANUFACTURER	CALIBER/GAUGE	QUANTITY	DATE

www.ingramcontent.com/pod-product-compliance
Lightning Source LLC
Chambersburg PA
CBHW071421070526
44578CB00003B/652